Introduction

The beginning of a new millennium fills us with hope. On the one hand, it is a milestone, a birthday, so to speak, that reminds us that the world really is changing. Like a birthday, it invites us to reflect on our past, imagine a better future and rise to a new level of maturity. On the other hand, the "millennium" is a reminder of "The Millennium" promised in the Bible – a thousand years of peace and the coming of the Kingdom of God on Earth. The Writings of the Bahá'í Faith invite us to bring these two visions of hope together. They put forth the argument that the Kingdom of God on Earth is not made of gold, pearls and gems, but is rather forged from the love, peace, and cooperation that is only possible when we demonstrate a level of collective maturity that was not possible in ages past.

This new level of maturity which we are striving towards is possible at this point in history only because God has been guiding us through each stage of our collective development for thousands of years. As we've matured, God has sent us new "teachers" – such as Abraham, Moses, Jesus and Mohammed. Each teacher renewed the spiritual teachings of the previous teacher, but changed the social teachings to meet the needs of an ever-advancing civilization.

The years preceding this millennium have been, like adolescence, a time of difficult transitions. We struggled to put an end to war and work together for the good of all humanity, but we also developed the ability to completely destroy ourselves. As we enter the new millennium, we also enter a new stage in our development — one in which it seems that almost anything has become possible. This new stage of growth requires new tools, new teachings and a new vision to guide us. God has met these needs though a new teacher, Bahá'u'lláh, Who fulfills the promises made by Christ by bringing us the spiritual blueprints, so to speak, for building the Kingdom of God on Earth.

About the Bahá'í Faith

The Bahá'í Faith is the newest, fastest growing and second most wide-spread of all of the world's major independent religions. It claims to be the most recent of God's revelations, uniquely designed to meet the needs of a rapidly maturing world.

It's Founder, Bahá'u'lláh (1817-1892), lived and taught during the very beginning of what we could call the modern age. Though He spent most of His life exiled, tortured and imprisoned by the most backward country of His age, He wrote thousands of letters and books outlining the path to a glorious new age of peace. This booklet offers just a sampling of His writings, and those of His son, 'Abdu'l-Bahá, His authorized interpreter. If you take a few moments to visualize the world that His inspiring, transforming, and challenging teachings describe, you will see that this new millennium could be very hopeful indeed.

BAHÁ'Í Teachings for a new Millennium

The potentialities inherent in the
station of man, the full measure of
his destiny on earth,
the innate excellence of his reality,
must all be manifested in this
promised Day of God.

Bahá'u'lláh

BAHÁ'Í
Teachings for a New Millennium

The quotations in this book represent a tiny fraction
of the available English translations of
the Bahá'í Sacred Writings.
They were selected from a variety of
authorized translations.
For a list of references, send a SASE to the publisher.

Published by Special Ideas
PO Box 9
Heltonville, IN 47436
1-800-326-1197

Compiled by Karen and Justice St. Rain
Cover design by Justice St. Rain

ISBN 1-888547-06-5

Printed in the USA

04 03 02 01   6 5 4 3 2

BUILDING A NEW RELATIONSHIP WITH GOD	1
God's Love for Us	1
Our Love for God	4
SPIRITUAL MATURITY	6
Understanding Who We Are	6
Created in God's Image	6
The Nature of the Soul	8
The Question of Good & Evil	10
The Afterlife	12
Developing Our Virtues	15
Growing Through Tests	17
TOOLS FOR SOCIAL PROGRESS	18
Loving Each Other	18
Eliminating Prejudice	20
Promoting Peace	22
Supporting Families	25
Supporting Women	28
Encouraging Education	29
Work Is Worship	32
Sharing Wealth	33
Seeking the Truth	35
Uniting Science & Religion	37
Improving Communication	40
THE ROLE OF RELIGION	41
Teaching Us About God	41
Seeking a Unifying Faith	42
Spiritual vs. Social Teachings	44
Prophets Are Teachers & Physicians	45
Recognizing the Prophets	47
Bahá'u'lláh Brings a New Message	49
ENVISIONING THE FUTURE	50
A Selection of Bahá'í Prayers	52

BUILDING A NEW RELATIONSHIP WITH GOD

God's Love for Us

♦ O SON OF MAN! Veiled in My immemorial being and in the ancient eternity of My essence, I knew My love for thee; therefore I created thee, have engraved on thee Mine image and revealed to thee My beauty.

Bahá'u'lláh

♦ O SON OF MAN! I loved thy creation, hence I created thee. Wherefore, do thou love Me, that I may name thy name and fill thy soul with the spirit of life.

Bahá'u'lláh

♦ O SON OF THE WONDROUS VISION! I have breathed within thee a breath of My own Spirit, that thou mayest be My lover. Why hast thou forsaken Me and sought a beloved other than Me?

Bahá'u'lláh

♦ O SON OF BOUNTY! Out of the wastes of nothingness, with the clay of My command I made thee to appear, and have ordained for thy training every atom in existence and the essence of all created things. Thus, ere thou didst issue from thy mother's womb, I destined for thee two founts of gleaming milk, eyes to watch over thee, and hearts to love thee. Out of My loving-kindness, 'neath the shade of My mercy I nurtured thee, and guarded thee by the essence of My grace and favor. And My purpose in all this was that thou mightest attain My everlasting dominion and become worthy of My invisible bestowals. And yet heedless thou didst remain, and when fully grown, thou didst neglect all My bounties and occupied thyself with thine idle imaginings, in such wise that thou didst become wholly forgetful, and, turning away from the portals of the Friend didst abide within the courts of My enemy. *Bahá'u'lláh*

♦ The good pleasure of God is love for His creatures. The will and plan of God is that each individual member of humankind shall become illumined like unto a lamp, radiant with all the destined virtues of humanity, leading his fellow creatures out of natural darkness into the heavenly light. Therein rests the virtue and glory of the world of humanity. This is the perfection, honor and glory of man; otherwise, man is an animal and without differentiation from the creatures of that lower kingdom. *'Abdu'l-Bahá*

♦ What a power is love! It is the most wonderful, the greatest of all living powers.

Love gives life to the lifeless. Love lights a flame in the heart that is cold. Love brings hope to the hopeless and gladdens the hearts of the sorrowful.

In the world of existence there is indeed no greater power than the power of love. When the heart of man is aglow with the flame of love, he is ready to sacrifice all — even his life. In the Gospel it is said God is love.

There are four kinds of love. The first is the love that flows from God to man; it consists of the inexhaustible graces, the Divine effulgence and heavenly illumination. Through this love the world of being receives life. Through this love man is endowed with physical existence, until, through the breath of the Holy Spirit – this same love – he receives eternal life and becomes the image of the Living God. This love is the origin of all the love in the world of creation.

The second is the love that flows from man to God. This is faith, attraction to the Divine, enkindlement, progress, entrance into the Kingdom of God, receiving the Bounties of God, illumination with the lights of the Kingdom. This love is the origin of all philanthropy; this love causes the hearts of men to reflect the rays of the Sun of Reality.   *'Abdu'l-Bahá*

A Prayer

O God! Refresh and gladden my spirit. Purify my heart. Illumine my powers. I lay all my affairs in Thy hand. Thou art my Guide and my Refuge. I will no longer be sorrowful and grieved; I will be a happy and joyful being. O God! I will no longer be full of anxiety, nor will I let trouble harass me. I will not dwell on the unpleasant things of life.

O God! Thou art more friend to me than I am to myself. I dedicate myself to Thee, O Lord.

'Abdu'l-Bahá

Our Love for God

♦ O SON OF BEING! Love Me, that I may love thee. If thou lovest Me not, My love can in no wise reach thee. Know this, O servant. *Bahá'u'lláh*

♦ That which beseemeth you is the love of God, and the love of Him Who is the Manifestation of His Essence, and the observance of whatsoever He chooseth to prescribe unto you, did ye but know it.
Bahá'u'lláh

♦ O My servants! Deprive not yourselves of the unfading and resplendent Light that shineth within the Lamp of Divine glory. Let the flame of the love of God burn brightly within your radiant hearts. Feed it with the oil of Divine guidance, and protect it within the shelter of your constancy. Guard it within the globe of trust and detachment from all else but God, so that the evil whisperings of the ungodly may not extinguish its light. *Bahá'u'lláh*

♦ Do you realize how much you should thank God for His blessings? If you should thank Him a thousand times with each breath, it would not be sufficient because God has created and trained you. He has protected you from every affliction and prepared every gift and bestowal. Consider what a kind Father He is. He bestows His gift before you ask. We were not in the world of existence, but as soon as we were born, we found everything prepared for our needs and comfort without question on our part. He has given us a kind father and compassionate mother, provided for us two springs of salubrious milk, pure atmosphere, refreshing water, gentle breezes and the sun shining above our heads. In brief, He has supplied all the necessities of life although we did not ask for any of these great gifts. With pure mercy and bounty He has prepared this great table. It is a mercy which precedes asking. *'Abdu'l-Bahá*

♦ The earth is in motion and growth; the mountains, hills and prairies are green and pleasant; the bounty is overflowing; the mercy universal; the rain is descending from the cloud of mercy; the brilliant Sun is shining; the full moon is ornamenting the horizon of ether; the great ocean-tide is flooding every little stream; the gifts are successive; the favors consecutive; and the refreshing breeze is blowing, wafting the fragrant perfume of the blossoms. Boundless treasure is in the hand of the King of Kings! Lift the hem of thy garment in order to receive it.

If we are not happy and joyous at this season, for what other season shall we wait and for what other time shall we look? *'Abdu'l-Bahá*

SPIRITUAL MATURITY

UNDERSTANDING WHO WE ARE
Created in God's Image

♦ O SON OF SPIRIT! I created thee rich, why dost thou bring thyself down to poverty? Noble I made thee, wherewith dost thou abase thyself? Out of the essence of knowledge I gave thee being, why seekest thou enlightenment from anyone beside Me? Out of the clay of love I molded thee, how dost thou busy thyself with another? Turn thy sight unto thyself, that thou mayest find Me standing within thee, mighty, powerful and self-subsisting. *Bahá'u'lláh*

♦ Whatever is in the heavens and whatever is on the earth is a direct evidence of the revelation within it of the attributes and names of God, inasmuch as within every atom are enshrined the signs that bear eloquent testimony to the revelation of that Most Great Light. Methinks, but for the potency of that revelation, no being could ever exist. How resplendent the luminaries of knowledge that shine in an atom, and how vast the oceans of wisdom that surge within a drop! To a supreme degree is this true of man, who, among all created things, hath been invested with the robe of such gifts, and hath been singled out for the glory of such distinction. For in him are potentially revealed all the attributes and names of God to a degree that no other created being hath excelled or surpassed. All these names and attributes are applicable to him.

Even as He hath said: "Man is My mystery, and I am his mystery." Manifold are the verses that have been repeatedly revealed in all the Heavenly Books and the Holy Scriptures, expressive of this most subtle and lofty theme. Even as He hath revealed: "We will surely show them Our signs in the world and within themselves." Again He saith: "And also in your own selves: will ye not, then, behold the signs of God?" And yet again He revealeth: "And be ye not like those who forget God, and whom He hath therefore caused to forget their own selves." In this connection, He Who is the eternal King – may the souls of all that dwell within the mystic Tabernacle be a sacrifice unto Him – hath spoken: "He hath known God who hath known himself." *Bahá'u'lláh*

♦ The station of man is great, very great. God has created man after His own image and likeness. He has endowed him with a mighty power which is capable of discovering the mysteries of phenomena. Through its use man is able to arrive at ideal conclusions instead of being restricted to the mere plane of sense impressions. As he possesses sense endowment in common with the animals, it is evident that he is distinguished above them by his conscious power of penetrating abstract realities. He acquires divine wisdom; he searches out the mysteries of creation; he witnesses the radiance of omnipotence; he attains the second birth – that is to say, he is born out of the material world just as he is born of the mother; he attains to everlasting life; he draws nearer to God; his heart is replete with the love of God. *'Abdu'l-Bahá*

The Nature of the Soul

♦ O SON OF BEING! Thou art My lamp and My light is in thee. Get thou from it thy radiance and seek none other than Me. For I have created thee rich and have bountifully shed My favor upon thee.

Bahá'u'lláh

♦ Having created the world and all that liveth and moveth therein, He, through the direct operation of His unconstrained and sovereign Will, chose to confer upon man the unique distinction and capacity to know Him and to love Him — a capacity that must needs be regarded as the generating impulse and the primary purpose underlying the whole of creation.... Upon the inmost reality of each and every created thing He hath shed the light of one of His names, and made it a recipient of the glory of one of His attributes. Upon the reality of man, however, He hath focused the radiance of all of His names and attributes, and made it a mirror of His own Self. Alone of all created things man hath been singled out for so great a favor, so enduring a bounty.

These energies with which the Day Star of Divine bounty and Source of heavenly guidance hath endowed the reality of man lie, however, latent within him, even as the flame is hidden within the candle and the rays of light are potentially present in the lamp. The radiance of these energies may be obscured by worldly desires even as the light of the sun can be concealed beneath the dust and dross which cover the mirror. Neither the candle nor the lamp can be lighted through their own unaided efforts, nor can it ever be possible for the mirror to free itself from its dross. It is clear and evident that until a fire is kindled the lamp will never be ignited, and unless the dross is blotted out from the face of the mirror it can never represent the image of the sun nor reflect its light and glory. *Bahá'u'lláh*

♦ And now, concerning thy question regarding the creation of man. Know thou that all men have been created in the nature made by God, the Guardian, the Self-Subsisting. Unto each one hath been prescribed a pre-ordained measure, as decreed in God's mighty and guarded Tablets. All that which ye potentially possess can, however, be manifested only as a result of your own volition. Your own acts testify to this truth. *Bahá'u'lláh*

♦ God has created man lofty and noble, made him a dominant factor in creation. He has specialized man with supreme bestowals, conferred upon him mind, perception, memory, abstraction and the powers of the senses. These gifts of God to man were intended to make him the manifestation of divine virtues, a radiant light in the world of creation, a source of life and the agency of constructiveness in the infinite fields of existence. *'Abdu'l-Bahá*

"What is the purpose of our lives?"
"To acquire virtues." *–'Abdu'l-Bahá*

The Question of Good & Evil

♦ O SON OF BEING! With the hands of power I made thee and with the fingers of strength I created thee; and within thee have I placed the essence of My light. Be thou content with it and seek naught else, for My work is perfect and My command is binding. Question it not, nor have a doubt thereof.
Bahá'u'lláh

♦ In creation there is no evil; all is good. Certain qualities and natures innate in some men and apparently blameworthy are not so in reality. For example, from the beginning of his life you can see in a nursing child the signs of greed, of anger and of temper. Then, it may be said, good and evil are innate in the reality of man, and this is contrary to the pure goodness of nature and creation. The answer to this is that greed, which is to ask for something more, is a praiseworthy quality provided that it is used suitably. So if a man is greedy to acquire science and knowledge, or to become compassionate, generous and just, it is most praiseworthy. If he exercises his anger and wrath against the bloodthirsty tyrants who are like ferocious beasts, it is very praiseworthy; but if he does not use these qualities in a right way, they are blameworthy.

Then it is evident that in creation and nature evil does not exist at all; but when the natural qualities of man are used in an unlawful way, they are blameworthy. So if a rich and generous person gives a sum of money to a poor man for his own necessities, and if the poor man spends that sum of money on unlawful things, that will be blameworthy. It is the same with all the natural qualities of man, which constitute the capital of life; if they be used and displayed in an unlawful way, they become blameworthy. Therefore, it is clear that creation is purely good. Consider that the worst of qualities and most odious of attributes, which is the foundation of all evil, is lying.... Notwithstanding all this, if a doctor consoles a sick man by saying, "Thank God you are better, and there is hope of your recovery," though these words are contrary to the truth, yet they may become the consolation of the patient and the turning point of the illness. This is not blameworthy. *'Abdu'l-Bahá*

♦ Necessarily there will be some who are defective amongst men, but it is our duty to enable them by kind methods of guidance and teaching to become perfected. Some will be found who are morally sick; they should be treated in order that they may be healed. Others are immature and like children; they must be trained and educated so that they may become wise and mature. Those who are asleep must be awakened; the indifferent must become mindful and attentive. But all this must be accomplished in the spirit of kindness and love and not by strife, antagonism nor in a spirit of hostility and hatred, for this is contrary to the good pleasure of God. That which is acceptable in the sight of God is love. Love is, in reality, the first effulgence of Divinity and the greatest splendor of God. *'Abdu'l-Bahá*

The Afterlife

♦ And now concerning thy question regarding the soul of man and its survival after death. Know thou of a truth that the soul, after its separation from the body, will continue to progress until it attaineth the presence of God, in a state and condition which neither the revolution of ages and centuries, nor the changes and chances of this world, can alter. It will endure as long as the Kingdom of God, His sovereignty, His dominion and power will endure. It will manifest the signs of God and His attributes, and will reveal His loving-kindness and bounty. The movement of My Pen is stilled when it attempteth to befittingly describe the loftiness and glory of so exalted a station.... The Prophets and Messengers of God have been sent down for the sole purpose of guiding mankind to the straight Path of Truth. The purpose underlying Their revelation hath been to educate all men, that they may, at the hour of death, ascend, in the utmost purity and sanctity and with absolute detachment, to the throne of the Most High.

Bahá'u'lláh

♦ The nature of the soul after death can never be described, nor is it meet and permissible to reveal its whole character to the eyes of men.... The world beyond is as different from this world as this world is different from that of the child while still in the womb of its mother. When the soul attaineth the Presence of God, it will assume the form that best befitteth its immortality and is worthy of its celestial habitation. *Bahá'u'lláh*

♦ Thou hast asked Me whether man, as apart from the Prophets of God and His chosen ones, will retain, after his physical death, the self-same individuality, personality, consciousness, and understanding that characterize his life in this world....

Know thou that the soul of man is exalted above, and is independent of all infirmities of body or mind. That a sick person showeth signs of weakness is due to the hindrances that interpose themselves between his soul and his body, for the soul itself remaineth unaffected by any bodily ailments. Consider the light of the lamp. Though an external object may interfere with its radiance, the light itself continueth to shine with undiminished power. In like manner, every malady afflicting the body of man is an impediment that preventeth the soul from manifesting its inherent might and power. When it leaveth the body, however, it will evince such ascendancy, and reveal such influence as no force on earth can equal. Every pure, every refined and sanctified soul will be endowed with tremendous power, and shall rejoice with exceeding gladness. *Bahá'u'lláh*

♦ For the life of the flesh is common to both men and animals, whereas the life of the spirit is possessed only by the pure in heart who have quaffed from the ocean of faith and partaken of the fruit of certitude. This life knoweth no death, and this existence is crowned by immortality. Even as it hath been said: "He who is a true believer liveth both in this world and in the world to come." If by "life" be meant this earthly life, it is evident that death must needs overtake it. *Bahá'u'lláh*

♦ It is clear and evident that all men shall, after their physical death, estimate the worth of their deeds, and realize all that their hands have wrought.

Bahá'u'lláh

♦ When we find truth, constancy, fidelity, and love, we are happy; but if we meet with lying, faithlessness, and deceit, we are miserable.

These are all things pertaining to the soul, and are not bodily ills. Thus, it is apparent that the soul, even as the body, has its own individuality. But if the body undergoes a change, the spirit need not be touched. When you break a glass on which the sun shines, the glass is broken, but the sun still shines! If a cage containing a bird is destroyed, the bird is unharmed! If a lamp is broken, the flame can still burn bright!

The same thing applies to the spirit of man. Though death destroy his body, it has no power over his spirit — this is eternal, everlasting, both birthless and deathless.

As to the soul of man after death, it remains in the degree of purity to which it has evolved during life in the physical body, and after it is freed from the body it remains plunged in the ocean of God's Mercy.

From the moment the soul leaves the body and arrives in the Heavenly World, its evolution is spiritual, and that evolution is: The approaching unto God.

'Abdu'l-Bahá

DEVELOPING OUR VIRTUES

♦ The Purpose of the one true God, exalted be His glory, in revealing Himself unto men is to lay bare those gems that lie hidden within the mine of their true and inmost selves. *Bahá'u'lláh*

♦ All men have been created to carry forward an ever-advancing civilization. The Almighty beareth Me witness: To act like the beasts of the field is unworthy of man. Those virtues that befit his dignity are forbearance, mercy, compassion and loving-kindness towards all the peoples and kindreds of the earth. Say: O friends! Drink your fill from this crystal stream that floweth through the heavenly grace of Him Who is the Lord of Names. Let others partake of its waters in My name, that the leaders of men in every land may fully recognize the purpose for which the Eternal Truth hath been revealed, and the reason for which they themselves have been created. *Bahá'u'lláh*

♦ Be generous in prosperity, and thankful in adversity. Be worthy of the trust of thy neighbor, and look upon him with a bright and friendly face. Be a treasure to the poor, an admonisher to the rich, an answerer of the cry of the needy, a preserver of the sanctity of thy pledge. Be fair in thy judgment, and guarded in thy speech. Be unjust to no man, and show all meekness to all men. Be as a lamp unto them that walk in darkness, a joy to the sorrowful, a sea for the thirsty, a haven for the distressed, an upholder and defender of the victim of oppression. Let integrity and uprightness

distinguish all thine acts. Be a home for the stranger, a balm to the suffering, a tower of strength for the fugitive. Be eyes to the blind, and a guiding light unto the feet of the erring. Be an ornament to the countenance of truth, a crown to the brow of fidelity, a pillar of the temple of righteousness, a breath of life to the body of mankind, an ensign of the hosts of justice, a luminary above the horizon of virtue, a dew to the soil of the human heart, an ark on the ocean of knowledge, a sun in the heaven of bounty, a gem on the diadem of wisdom, a shining light in the firmament of thy generation, a fruit upon the tree of humility.
Bahá'u'lláh

♦ But the spirit of man has two aspects: one divine, one satanic — that is to say, it is capable of the utmost perfection, or it is capable of the utmost imperfection. If it acquires virtues, it is the most noble of the existing beings; and if it acquires vices, it becomes the most degraded existence. *'Abdu'l-Bahá*

♦ Therefore, we learn that nearness to God is possible through devotion to Him, through entrance into the Kingdom and service to humanity; it is attained by unity with mankind and through loving-kindness to all; it is dependent upon investigation of truth, acquisition of praiseworthy virtues, service in the cause of universal peace and personal sanctification. In a word, nearness to God necessitates sacrifice of self, severance and the giving up of all to Him. Nearness is likeness. *'Abdu'l-Bahá*

Growing through Tests

♦ O SON OF MAN! My calamity is My providence, outwardly it is fire and vengeance, but inwardly it is light and mercy. Hasten thereunto that thou mayest become an eternal light and an immortal spirit. This is My command unto thee, do thou observe it.

Bahá'u'lláh

♦ The more difficulties one sees in the world the more perfect one becomes. The more you plough and dig the ground the more fertile it becomes. The more you put the gold in the fire the purer it becomes. The more you sharpen the steel by grinding the better it cuts. Therefore, the more sorrows one sees the more perfect one becomes. That is why, in all times, the Prophets of God have had tribulations and difficulties to withstand. The more often the captain of a ship is in the tempest and difficult sailing the greater his knowledge becomes. Therefore I am happy that you have had great tribulations and difficulties. For this I am very happy – that you have had many sorrows. Strange it is that I love you and still I am happy that you have sorrows.

'Abdu'l-Bahá

♦ Men who suffer not, attain no perfection. The plant most pruned by the gardeners is that one which, when the summer comes, will have the most beautiful blossoms and the most abundant fruit.

'Abdu'l-Bahá

TOOLS FOR SOCIAL PROGRESS

LOVING EACH OTHER

♦ Ye are the fruits of one tree, and the leaves of one branch. Deal ye one with another with the utmost love and harmony, with friendliness and fellowship. He Who is the Day-Star of Truth beareth Me witness! So powerful is the light of unity that it can illuminate the whole earth. *Bahá'u'lláh*

♦ O FRIEND! In the garden of thy heart plant naught but the rose of love, and from the nightingale of affection and desire loosen not thy hold. Treasure the companionship of the righteous and eschew all fellowship with the ungodly. *Bahá'u'lláh*

♦ Wish not for others what ye wish not for yourselves; fear God, and be not of the prideful. Ye are all created out of water, and unto dust shall ye return. Reflect upon the end that awaiteth you, and walk not in the ways of the oppressor.

Bahá'u'lláh

♦ The earth is but one country, and mankind its citizens. *Bahá'u'lláh*

♦ God has created His servants in order that they may love and associate with each other. He has revealed the glorious splendor of His sun of love in the world of humanity. The cause of the creation of the phenomenal world is love. *'Abdu'l-Bahá*

◆ God desires unity and love; He commands harmony and fellowship. Enmity is human disobedience; God Himself is love. *'Abdu'l-Bahá*

◆ . . . man should be willing to accept hardships for himself in order that others may enjoy wealth; he should enjoy trouble for himself that others may enjoy happiness and well-being. This is the attribute of man. This is becoming of man. Otherwise man is not man – he is less than the animal. *'Abdu'l-Bahá*

◆ Strive day and night that animosity and contention may pass away from the hearts of men, that all religions shall become reconciled and the nations love each other so that no racial, religious or political prejudice may remain and the world of humanity behold God as the beginning and end of all existence. God has created all, and all return to God. Therefore, love humanity with all your heart and soul. If you meet a poor man, assist him; if you see the sick, heal him; reassure the affrighted one, render the cowardly noble and courageous, educate the ignorant, associate with the stranger. Emulate God. Consider how kindly, how lovingly He deals with all, and follow His example. *'Abdu'l-Bahá*

◆ Consider how kind Jesus Christ was, that even upon the cross He prayed for His oppressors. We must follow His example. We must emulate the Prophets of God. We must follow Jesus Christ. We must free ourselves from all these imitations which are the source of darkness in the world. *'Abdu'l-Bahá*

ELIMINATING PREJUDICE

♦ O CHILDREN OF MEN! Know ye not why We created you all from the same dust? That no one should exalt himself over the other. Ponder at all times in your hearts how ye were created. Since We have created you all from one same substance it is incumbent on you to be even as one soul, to walk with the same feet, eat with the same mouth and dwell in the same land, that from your inmost being, by your deeds and actions, the signs of oneness and the essence of detachment may be made manifest. Such is My counsel to you, O concourse of light! Heed ye this counsel that ye may obtain the fruit of holiness from the tree of wondrous glory. *Bahá'u'lláh*

♦ . . . prejudice – whether it be religious, racial, patriotic or political in its origin and aspect – is the destroyer of human foundations and opposed to the commands of God. *'Abdu'l-Bahá*

♦ And the breeding-ground of all these tragedies is prejudice: prejudice of race and nation, of religion, of political opinion; and the root cause of prejudice is blind imitation of the past – imitation in religion, in racial attitudes, in national bias, in politics. So long as this aping of the past persisteth, just so long will the foundations of the social order be blown to the four winds, just so long will humanity be continually exposed to direst peril. *'Abdu'l-Bahá*

♦ But there is need of a superior power to overcome human prejudices, a power which nothing in the world of mankind can withstand and which will overshadow the effect of all other forces at work in human conditions. That irresistible power is the love of God. It is my hope and prayer that it may destroy the prejudice of this one point of distinction between you and unite you all permanently under its hallowed protection.
'Abdu'l-Bahá

♦ Your eyes have been illumined, your ears are attentive, your hearts knowing. You must be free from prejudice and fanaticism, beholding no differences between the races and religions. You must look to God, for He is the real Shepherd, and all humanity are His sheep. He loves them and loves them equally. As this is true, should the sheep quarrel among themselves? They should manifest gratitude and thankfulness to God, and the best way to thank God is to love one another.   *'Abdu'l-Bahá*

♦ O Thou Provider! The dearest wish of this servant of Thy Threshold is to behold the friends of East and West in close embrace; to see all the members of human society gathered with love in a single great assemblage, even as individual drops of water collected in one mighty sea; to behold them all as birds in one garden of roses, as pearls of one ocean, as leaves of one tree, as rays of one sun....   *'Abdu'l-Bahá*

PROMOTING PEACE

♦ The third teaching of Bahá'u'lláh concerns universal peace among the nations, among the religions, among the races and native lands. He has declared that so long as prejudice — whether religious, racial, patriotic, political or sectarian — continues to exist among mankind, universal peace cannot become a reality in the world. From the earliest history of man down to the present time all the wars and bloodshed which have taken place were caused either by religious, racial, political or sectarian bias. Therefore, it is evident that so long as these prejudices continue, the world of humanity cannot attain peace and composure. *'Abdu'l-Bahá*

♦ All mankind are creatures and servants of the one God. The surface of the earth is one home; humanity is one family and household. Distinctions and boundaries are artificial, human. Why should there be discord and strife among men? All must become united and coordinated in service to the world of humanity. *'Abdu'l-Bahá*

♦ In the days of old an instinct for warfare was developed in the struggle with wild animals; this is no longer necessary; nay, rather, co-operation and mutual understanding are seen to produce the greatest welfare of mankind. Enmity is now the result of prejudice only. *'Abdu'l-Bahá*

♦ History shows that throughout the past there has been continual warfare and strife among the various nations, peoples and sects; but now – praise be to God! – in this century of illumination, hearts are inclined toward agreement and fellowship, and minds are thoughtful upon the question of the unification of mankind. There is an emanation of the universal consciousness today which clearly indicates the dawn of a great unity. *'Abdu'l-Bahá*

♦ True civilization will unfurl its banner in the midmost heart of the world whenever a certain number of its distinguished and high-minded sovereigns – the shining exemplars of devotion and determination – shall, for the good and happiness of all mankind, arise, with firm resolve and clear vision, to establish the Cause of Universal Peace. They must make the Cause of Peace the object of general consultation, and seek by every means in their power to establish a Union of the nations of the world. *'Abdu'l-Bahá*

♦ The world is in greatest need of international peace. Until it is established, mankind will not attain composure and tranquillity. It is necessary that the nations and governments organize an international tribunal to which all their disputes and differences shall be referred. The decision of that tribunal shall be final. Individual controversy will be adjudged by a local tribunal. International questions will come before the universal tribunal, and so the cause of warfare will be taken away. *'Abdu'l-Bahá*

♦ Universal peace is an impossibility through human and material agencies; it must be through spiritual power. There is need of a universal impelling force which will establish the oneness of humanity and destroy the foundations of war and strife. None other than the divine power can do this; therefore, it will be accomplished through the breath of the Holy Spirit.
'Abdu'l-Bahá

♦ When love is realized and the ideal spiritual bonds unite the hearts of men, the whole human race will be uplifted, the world will continually grow more spiritual and radiant and the happiness and tranquillity of mankind be immeasurably increased. Warfare and strife will be uprooted, disagreement and dissension pass away and universal peace unite the nations and peoples of the world. *'Abdu'l-Bahá*

♦ Consider the harmful effect of discord and dissension in a family; then reflect upon the favors and blessings which descend upon that family when unity exists among its various members. What incalculable benefits and blessings would descend upon the great human family if unity and brotherhood were established! In this century when the beneficent results of unity and the ill effects of discord are so clearly apparent, the means for the attainment and accomplishment of human fellowship have appeared in the world. Bahá'u'lláh has proclaimed and provided the way by which hostility and dissension may be removed from the human world. He has left no ground or possibility for strife and disagreement. *'Abdu'l-Bahá*

Supporting Families

♦ My home is the home of peace. My home is the home of joy and delight. My home is the home of laughter and exultation. Whosoever enters through the portals of this home, must go out with gladsome heart. This is the home of light; whosoever enters here must become illumined.... *'Abdu'l-Bahá*

♦ The friends of God must so live and conduct themselves, and evince such excellence of character and conduct, as to make others astonished. The love between husband and wife must not be purely physical, nay, rather, it must be spiritual and heavenly.
'Abdu'l-Bahá

♦ In this glorious Cause the life of a married couple should resemble the life of the angels in heaven — a life full of joy and spiritual delight, a life of unity and concord, a friendship both mental and physical. The home should be orderly and well-organized. Their ideas and thoughts should be like the rays of the sun of truth and the radiance of the brilliant stars in the heavens. Even as two birds they should warble melodies upon the branches of the tree of fellowship and harmony. They should always be elated with joy and gladness and be a source of happiness to the hearts of others. They should set an example to their fellowmen, manifest a true and sincere love towards each other and educate their children in such a manner as to blazon the fame and glory of their family.
'Abdu'l-Bahá

♦ If thou wouldst show kindness and consideration to thy parents so that they may feel generally pleased, this would also please Me, for parents must be highly respected and it is essential that they should feel contented, . . . *'Abdu'l-Bahá*

♦ According to the teachings of Bahá'u'lláh the family, being a human unit, must be educated according to the rules of sanctity. All the virtues must be taught the family. The integrity of the family bond must be constantly considered, and the rights of the individual members must not be transgressed. The rights of the son, the father, the mother — none of them must be transgressed, none of them must be arbitrary. Just as the son has certain obligations to his father, the father, likewise, has certain obligations to his son. The mother, the sister and other members of the household have their certain prerogatives. All these rights and prerogatives must be conserved, yet the unity of the family must be sustained. The injury of one shall be considered the injury of all; the comfort of each, the comfort of all; the honor of one, the honor of all.
'Abdu'l-Bahá

♦ Note ye how easily, where unity existeth in a given family, the affairs of that family are conducted; what progress the members of that family make, how they prosper in the world. Their concerns are in order, they enjoy comfort and tranquillity, they are secure, their position is assured, they come to be envied by all. *'Abdu'l-Bahá*

♦ I beseech God to graciously make of thy home a center for the diffusion of the light of divine guidance, for the dissemination of the Words of God and for enkindling at all times the fire of love in the hearts of His faithful servants and maidservants. Know thou of a certainty that every house wherein the anthem of praise is raised to the Realm of Glory in celebration of the Name of God is indeed a heavenly home, and one of the gardens of delight in the Paradise of God.

'Abdu'l-Bahá

♦ Treat all thy friends and relatives, even strangers, with a spirit of utmost love and kindliness.

'Abdu'l-Bahá

A Prayer for Families

Thou seest, O Lord, our suppliant hands lifted up towards the heaven of Thy favor and bounty. Grant that they may be filled with the treasures of Thy munificence and bountiful favor. Forgive us, and our fathers, and our mothers, and fulfil whatsoever we have desired from the ocean of Thy grace and Divine generosity. Accept, O Beloved of our hearts, all our works in Thy path. Thou art, verily, the Most Powerful, the Most Exalted, the Incomparable, the One, the Forgiving, the Gracious.

Bahá'u'lláh

SUPPORTING WOMEN

♦ Women and men have been and will always be equal in the sight of God. The Dawning-Place of the Light of God sheddeth its radiance upon all with the same effulgence. Verily God created women for men, and men for women. *Bahá'u'lláh*

♦ And among the teachings of Bahá'u'lláh is the equality of women and men. The world of humanity has two wings – one is women and the other men. Not until both wings are equally developed can the bird fly. Should one wing remain weak, flight is impossible. Not until the world of women becomes equal to the world of men in the acquisition of virtues and perfections, can success and prosperity be attained as they ought to be. *'Abdu'l-Bahá*

♦ Woman's lack of progress and proficiency has been due to her need of equal education and opportunity. Had she been allowed this equality, there is no doubt she would be the counterpart of man in ability and capacity. The happiness of mankind will be realized when women and men coordinate and advance equally, for each is the complement and helpmeet of the other. *'Abdu'l-Bahá*

♦ Women shall receive an equal privilege of education. This will enable them to qualify and progress in all degrees of occupation and accomplishment.
'Abdu'l-Bahá

♦ Women have equal rights with men upon earth; in religion and society they are a very important element. As long as women are prevented from attaining their highest possibilities, so long will men be unable to achieve the greatness which might be theirs.   *'Abdu'l-Bahá*

♦ In this day there are women among the Bahá'ís who far outshine men. They are wise, talented, well-informed, progressive, most intelligent and the light of men. They surpass men in courage. When they speak in meetings, the men listen with great respect. Furthermore, the education of women is of greater importance than the education of men, for they are the mothers of the race, and mothers rear the children. The first teachers of children are the mothers. Therefore, they must be capably trained in order to educate both sons and daughters.   *'Abdu'l-Bahá*

ENCOURAGING EDUCATION

♦ Man is the supreme Talisman. Lack of a proper education hath, however, deprived him of that which he doth inherently possess. Through a word proceeding out of the mouth of God he was called into being; by one word more he was guided to recognize the Source of his education; by yet another word his station and destiny were safeguarded. The Great Being saith: Regard man as a mine rich in gems of inestimable value. Education can, alone, cause it to reveal its treasures, and enable mankind to benefit therefrom.   *Bahá'u'lláh*

♦ Among other teachings and principles Bahá'u'lláh counsels the education of all members of society. No individual should be denied or deprived of intellectual training, although each should receive according to capacity. None must be left in the grades of ignorance, for ignorance is a defect in the human world. All mankind must be given a knowledge of science and philosophy – that is, as much as may be deemed necessary. All cannot be scientists and philosophers, but each should be educated according to his needs and deserts. *'Abdu'l-Bahá*

♦ Let the mothers consider that whatever concerneth the education of children is of the first importance. Let them put forth every effort in this regard, for when the bough is green and tender it will grow in whatever way ye train it. Therefore is it incumbent upon the mothers to rear their little ones even as a gardener tendeth his young plants. Let them strive by day and by night to establish within their children faith and certitude, the fear of God, the love of the Beloved of the worlds, and all good qualities and traits. Whensoever a mother seeth that her child hath done well, let her praise and applaud him and cheer his heart; and if the slightest undesirable trait should manifest itself, let her counsel the child and punish him, and use means based on reason, even a slight verbal chastisement should this be necessary. It is not, however, permissible to strike a child, or vilify him, for the child's character will be totally perverted if he be subjected to blows or verbal abuse. *'Abdu'l-Bahá*

♦ But education is of three kinds: material, human and spiritual. Material education is concerned with the progress and development of the body, through gaining its sustenance, its material comfort and ease. This education is common to animals and man.

Human education signifies civilization and progress — that is to say, government, administration, charitable works, trades, arts and handicrafts, sciences, great inventions and discoveries and elaborate institutions, which are the activities essential to man as distinguished from the animal.

Divine education is that of the Kingdom of God: it consists in acquiring divine perfections, and this is true education; for in this state man becomes the focus of divine blessings, the manifestation of the words, "Let Us make man in Our image, and after Our likeness." This is the goal of the world of humanity.
'Abdu'l-Bahá

♦ It is evident, therefore, that man is in need of divine education and inspiration, that the spirit and bounties of God are essential to his development. That is to say, the teachings of Christ and the Prophets are necessary for his education and guidance. Why? Because They are the divine Gardeners Who till the earth of human hearts and minds. They educate man, uproot the weeds, burn the thorns and remodel the waste places into gardens and orchards where fruitful trees grow. The wisdom and purpose of Their training is that man must pass from degree to degree of progressive unfoldment until perfection is attained. *'Abdu'l-Bahá*

Work is Worship

♦ In addition to this wide-spread education each child must be taught a profession, art, or trade, so that every member of the community will be enabled to earn his own livelihood. Work done in the spirit of service is the highest form of worship....

'Abdu'l-Bahá

♦ This is worship: to serve mankind and to minister to the needs of the people. Service is prayer. A physician ministering to the sick, gently, tenderly, free from prejudice and believing in the solidarity of the human race, he is giving praise.

'Abdu'l-Bahá

♦ ...order your lives in accordance with the first principle of the divine teaching, which is love. Service to humanity is service to God. Let the love and light of the Kingdom radiate through you until all who look upon you shall be illumined by its reflection. Be as stars, brilliant and sparkling in the loftiness of their heavenly station.

'Abdu'l-Bahá

♦ It must not be implied that one should give up avocation and attainment to livelihood. On the contrary, in the Cause of Bahá'u'lláh monasticism and asceticism are not sanctioned. In this great Cause the light of guidance is shining and radiant. Bahá'u'lláh has even said that occupation and labor are devotion.

'Abdu'l-Bahá

Sharing Wealth

♦ O CHILDREN OF DUST! Tell the rich of the midnight sighing of the poor, lest heedlessness lead them into the path of destruction, and deprive them of the Tree of Wealth. To give and to be generous are attributes of Mine; well is it with him that adorneth himself with My virtues. *Bahá'u'lláh*

♦ O SON OF MAN! Bestow My wealth upon My poor, that in heaven thou mayest draw from stores of unfading splendor and treasures of imperishable glory.
Bahá'u'lláh

♦ The fourth principle or teaching of Bahá'u'lláh is the readjustment and equalization of the economic standards of mankind. This deals with the question of human livelihood. It is evident that under present systems and conditions of government the poor are subject to the greatest need and distress while others more fortunate live in luxury and plenty far beyond their actual necessities. This inequality of portion and privilege is one of the deep and vital problems of human society. That there is need of an equalization and apportionment by which all may possess the comforts and privileges of life is evident. The remedy must be legislative readjustment of conditions. The rich too must be merciful to the poor, contributing from willing hearts to their needs without being forced or compelled to do so. The composure of the world will be assured by the establishment of this principle in the religious life of mankind. *'Abdu'l-Bahá*

♦ The essence of the matter is that divine justice will become manifest in human conditions and affairs, and all mankind will find comfort and enjoyment in life.
'Abdu'l-Bahá

♦ Hearts must be so cemented together, love must become so dominant that the rich shall most willingly extend assistance to the poor and take steps to establish these economic adjustments permanently. If it is accomplished in this way, it will be most praiseworthy because then it will be for the sake of God and in the pathway of His service. For example, it will be as if the rich inhabitants of a city should say, "It is neither just nor lawful that we should possess great wealth while there is abject poverty in this community," and then willingly give their wealth to the poor, retaining only as much as will enable them to live comfortably.

Strive, therefore, to create love in the hearts in order that they may become glowing and radiant. When that love is shining, it will permeate other hearts even as this electric light illumines its surroundings. When the love of God is established, everything else will be realized. This is the true foundation of all economics. Reflect upon it. Endeavor to become the cause of the attraction of souls rather than to enforce minds. Manifest true economics to the people. Show what love is, what kindness is, what true severance is and generosity. This is the important thing for you to do. Act in accordance with the teachings of Bahá'u'lláh.
'Abdu'l-Bahá

SEEKING THE TRUTH

♦ Happy is the man that pondereth in his heart that which hath been revealed in the Books of God, the Help in Peril, the Self-Subsisting.   *Bahá'u'lláh*

♦ Blessed are the just souls who seek the truth.
'Abdu'l-Bahá

♦ God has given man the eye of investigation by which he may see and recognize truth. He has endowed man with ears that he may hear the message of reality and conferred upon him the gift of reason by which he may discover things for himself. This is his endowment and equipment for the investigation of reality. Man is not intended to see through the eyes of another, hear through another's ears nor comprehend with another's brain. Each human creature has individual endowment, power and responsibility in the creative plan of God. Therefore, depend upon your own reason and judgment and adhere to the outcome of your own investigation; otherwise, you will be utterly submerged in the sea of ignorance and deprived of all the bounties of God.   *'Abdu'l-Bahá*

♦ It is, therefore, clear that in order to make any progress in the search after truth we must relinquish superstition. If all seekers would follow this principle they would obtain a clear vision of the truth.

If five people meet together to seek for truth, they must begin by cutting themselves free from all their own special conditions and renouncing all preconceived ideas. In order to find truth we must give up our prejudices, our own small trivial notions; an open receptive mind is essential. If our chalice is full of self, there is no room in it for the water of life. The fact that we imagine ourselves to be right and everybody else wrong is the greatest of all obstacles in the path towards unity, and unity is necessary if we would reach truth, for truth is one.

Therefore it is imperative that we should renounce our own particular prejudices and superstitions if we earnestly desire to seek the truth. Unless we make a distinction in our minds between dogma, superstition and prejudice on the one hand, and truth on the other, we cannot succeed. When we are in earnest in our search for anything we look for it everywhere. This principle we must carry out in our search for truth.

Science must be accepted. No one truth can contradict another truth. Light is good in whatsoever lamp it is burning! A rose is beautiful in whatsoever garden it may bloom! A star has the same radiance if it shines from the East or from the West. Be free from prejudice, so will you love the Sun of Truth from whatsoever point in the horizon it may arise! You will realize that if the Divine light of truth shone in Jesus Christ it also shone in Moses and in Buddha. The earnest seeker will arrive at this truth. This is what is meant by the 'Search after Truth'.   *'Abdu'l-Bahá*

Uniting Science & Religion

♦ And among the teachings of Bahá'u'lláh is that religion must be in conformity with science and reason, so that it may influence the hearts of men. The foundation must be solid and must not consist of imitations.
'Abdu'l-Bahá

♦ Between scientists and the followers of religion there has always been controversy and strife for the reason that the latter have proclaimed religion superior in authority to science and considered scientific announcement opposed to the teachings of religion. Bahá'u'lláh declared that religion is in complete harmony with science and reason. If religious belief and doctrine is at variance with reason, it proceeds from the limited mind of man and not from God; therefore, it is unworthy of belief and not deserving of attention; the heart finds no rest in it, and real faith is impossible. How can man believe that which he knows to be opposed to reason? Is this possible? Can the heart accept that which reason denies? Reason is the first faculty of man, and the religion of God is in harmony with it. Bahá'u'lláh has removed this form of dissension and discord from among mankind and reconciled science with religion by revealing the pure teachings of the divine reality. This accomplishment is specialized to Him in this Day.
'Abdu'l-Bahá

♦ If the religious beliefs of mankind are contrary to science and opposed to reason, they are none other than superstitions and without divine authority, for the Lord God has endowed man with the faculty of reason in order that through its exercise he may arrive at the verities of existence. Reason is the discoverer of the realities of things, and that which conflicts with its conclusions is the product of human fancy and imagination.

'Abdu'l-Bahá

♦ If religion is opposed to reason and science, faith is impossible; and when faith and confidence in the divine religion are not manifest in the heart, there can be no spiritual attainment.

'Abdu'l-Bahá

♦ Religion must conform to science and reason; otherwise, it is superstition. God has created man in order that he may perceive the verity of existence and endowed him with mind or reason to discover truth. Therefore, scientific knowledge and religious belief must be conformable to the analysis of this divine faculty in man.

'Abdu'l-Bahá

♦ Man is always progressing. His circle of knowledge is ever widening, and his mental activity flows through many and varied channels. Look what man has accomplished in the field of science, consider his many discoveries and countless inventions and his profound understanding of natural law.

In the world of art it is just the same, and this wonderful development of man's faculties becomes more and more rapid as time goes on. If the discoveries, inventions and material accomplishments of the last fifteen hundred years could be put together, you would see that there has been greater advancement during the last hundred years than in the previous fourteen centuries. For the rapidity with which man is progressing increases century by century.

The power of the intellect is one of God's greatest gifts to men, it is the power that makes him a higher creature than the animal. For whereas, century by century and age by age man's intelligence grows and becomes keener, that of the animal remains the same. They are no more intelligent today then they were a thousand years ago! Is there a greater proof than this needed to show man's dissimilarity to the animal creation? It is surely as clear as day.

As for the spiritual perfections they are man's birthright and belong to him alone of all creation. Man is, in reality, a spiritual being, and only when he lives in the spirit is he truly happy.

'Abdu'l-Bahá

IMPROVING COMMUNICATION

♦ The day is approaching when all the peoples of the world will have adopted one universal language and one common script. When this is achieved, to whatsoever city a man may journey, it shall be as if he were entering his own home.

Bahá'u'lláh

♦ Bahá'u'lláh has proclaimed the adoption of a universal language. A language shall be agreed upon by which unity will be established in the world. Each person will require training in two languages: his native tongue and the universal auxiliary form of speech. This will facilitate intercommunication and dispel the misunderstandings which the barriers of language have occasioned in the world.

'Abdu'l-Bahá

♦ One of the great steps towards universal peace would be the establishment of a universal language.

'Abdu'l-Bahá

♦ Settle all things, both great and small, by consultation. Without prior consultation, take no important step in your own personal affairs. Concern yourselves with one another. Help along one another's projects and plans. Grieve over one another. Let none in the whole country go in need. Befriend one another until ye become as a single body, one and all….

'Abdu'l-Bahá

THE ROLE OF RELIGION

Teaching Us about God

♦ That which we imagine, is not the Reality of God; He, the Unknowable, the Unthinkable, is far beyond the highest conception of man.   *'Abdu'l-Bahá*

♦ To every discerning and illumined heart it is evident that God, the unknowable Essence, the divine Being, is immensely exalted beyond every human attribute, such as corporeal existence, ascent and descent, egress and regress. Far be it from His glory that human tongue should adequately recount His praise, or that human heart comprehend His fathomless mystery. He is and hath ever been veiled in the ancient eternity of His Essence, and will remain in His Reality everlastingly hidden from the sight of men....

The door of the knowledge of the Ancient of Days being thus closed in the face of all beings, the Source of infinite grace, according to His saying: "His grace hath transcended all things; My grace hath encompassed them all" hath caused those luminous Gems of Holiness [the Prophets] to appear out of the realm of the spirit, in the noble form of the human temple, and be made manifest unto all men, that they may impart unto the world the mysteries of the unchangeable Being, and tell of the subtleties of His imperishable Essence. These sanctified Mirrors, these Day-springs of ancient glory are one and all the Exponents on earth

of Him Who is the central Orb of the universe, its Essence and ultimate Purpose. From Him proceed their knowledge and power; from Him is derived their sovereignty. The beauty of their countenance is but a reflection of His image, and their revelation a sign of His deathless glory. They are the Treasuries of divine knowledge, and the Repositories of celestial wisdom. Through them is transmitted a grace that is infinite, and by them is revealed the light that can never fade.
Bahá'u'lláh

SEEKING A UNIFYING FAITH

♦ This is the changeless Faith of God, eternal in the past, eternal in the future. Let him that seeketh, attain it; and as to him that hath refused to seek it — verily, God is Self-Sufficient, above any need of His creatures. *Bahá'u'lláh*

♦ In thine esteemed letter thou hadst inquired which of the Prophets of God should be regarded as superior to others. Know thou assuredly that the essence of all the Prophets of God is one and the same. Their unity is absolute. God, the Creator, saith: There is no distinction whatsoever among the Bearers of My Message. They all have but one purpose; their secret is the same secret. To prefer one in honor to another, to exalt certain ones above the rest, is in no wise to be permitted. Every true Prophet hath regarded His Message as fundamentally the same as the Revelation of every other Prophet gone before Him. If any man, therefore, should fail to comprehend this truth, and should consequently indulge in vain and unseemly language, no one whose sight is keen and whose understanding is enlightened would ever allow such idle talk to cause him to waver in his belief.

The measure of the revelation of the Prophets of God in this world, however, must differ. Each and every one of them hath been the Bearer of a distinct Message, and hath been commissioned to reveal Himself through specific acts. It is for this reason that they appear to vary in their greatness. Their Revelation may be likened unto the light of the moon that sheddeth its radiance upon the earth. Though every time it appeareth, it revealeth a fresh measure of its brightness, yet its inherent splendor can never diminish, nor can its light suffer extinction. *Bahá'u'lláh*

♦ The foundation of all the divine religions is one. All are based upon reality. *'Abdu'l-Bahá*

♦ Blessed souls whether Moses, Jesus, Zoroaster, Krishna, Buddha, Confucius, or Muhammad were the cause of the illumination of the world of humanity. How can we deny such irrefutable proof? How can we be blind to such light? How can we dispute the validity of His Holiness Christ? This is injustice. This is a denial of reality. Man must be just. We must set aside bias and prejudice. We must abandon the imitations of ancestors and forefathers. We ourselves must investigate reality and be fair in judgment.
'Abdu'l-Bahá

◆ Therefore, if the religions investigate reality and seek the essential truth of their own foundations, they will agree and no difference will be found. But inasmuch as religions are submerged in dogmatic imitations, forsaking the original foundations, and as imitations differ widely, therefore, the religions are divergent and antagonistic. These imitations may be likened to clouds which obscure the sunrise; but reality is the sun. If the clouds disperse, the Sun of Reality shines upon all, and no difference of vision will exist. The religions will then agree, for fundamentally they are the same. The subject is one, but predicates are many.

'Abdu'l-Bahá

◆ All the teaching of the Prophets is one; one faith; one Divine light shining throughout the world. Now, under the banner of the oneness of humanity all people of all creeds should turn away from prejudice and become friends and believers in all the Prophets.

'Abdu'l-Bahá

Spiritual vs. Social Teachings

◆ Each of the divine religions embodies two kinds of ordinances. The first is those which concern spiritual susceptibilities, the development of moral principles and the quickening of the conscience of man. These are essential or fundamental, one and the same in all religions, changeless and eternal — reality not subject to transformation. Abraham heralded this reality, Moses promulgated it, and Jesus Christ established it in the world of mankind. All the divine Prophets and Messengers were the instruments and channels of this same eternal, essential truth.

The second kind of ordinances in the divine religions is those which relate to the material affairs of humankind. These are the material or accidental laws which are subject to change in each day of manifestation, according to exigencies of the time, conditions and differing capacities of humanity.   *'Abdu'l-Bahá*

Prophets Are Teachers & Physicians

♦ The Prophets and Messengers of God have been sent down for the sole purpose of guiding mankind to the straight Path of Truth. The purpose underlying Their revelation hath been to educate all men, that they may, at the hour of death, ascend, in the utmost purity and sanctity and with absolute detachment, to the throne of the Most High. The light which these souls radiate is responsible for the progress of the world and the advancement of its peoples. They are like unto leaven which leaveneth the world of being, and constitute the animating force through which the arts and wonders of the world are made manifest. Through them the clouds rain their bounty upon men, and the earth bringeth forth its fruits. All things must needs have a cause, a motive power, an animating principle. These souls and symbols of detachment have provided, and will continue to provide, the supreme moving impulse in the world of being.

Bahá'u'lláh

♦ The Prophets of God should be regarded as physicians whose task is to foster the well-being of the world and its peoples, that, through the spirit of oneness, they may heal the sickness of a divided humanity. To none is given the right to question their words or disparage their conduct, for they are the only ones who can claim to have understood the patient and to have correctly diagnosed its ailments. No man, however acute his perception, can ever hope to reach the heights which the wisdom and understanding of the Divine Physician have attained. Little wonder, then, if the treatment prescribed by the physician in this day should not be found to be identical with that which he prescribed before. How could it be otherwise when the ills affecting the sufferer necessitate at every stage of his sickness a special remedy? In like manner, every time the Prophets of God have illumined the world with the resplendent radiance of the Day Star of Divine knowledge, they have invariably summoned its peoples to embrace the light of God through such means as best befitted the exigencies of the age in which they appeared. They were thus able to scatter the darkness of ignorance, and to shed upon the world the glory of their own knowledge. It is towards the inmost essence of these Prophets, therefore, that the eye of every man of discernment must be directed, inasmuch as their one and only purpose hath always been to guide the erring, and give peace to the afflicted. *Bahá'u'lláh*

Recognizing the Prophets

♦ Beware lest any name debar you from Him Who is the Possessor of all names, or any word shut you out from this Remembrance of God, this Source of Wisdom amongst you. *Bahá'u'lláh*

♦ For example, we mention Abraham and Moses. By this mention we do not mean the limitation implied in the mere names but intend the virtues which these names embody. When we say Abraham, we mean thereby a manifestation of divine guidance, a center of human virtues, a source of heavenly bestowals to mankind, a dawning point of divine inspiration and perfections. These perfections and graces are not limited to names and boundaries. When we find these virtues, qualities and attributes in any personality, we recognize the same reality shining from within and bow in acknowledgment of the Abrahamic perfections. Similarly, we acknowledge and adore the beauty of Moses. Some souls were lovers of the name Abraham, loving the lantern instead of the light, and when they saw this same light shining from another lantern, they were so attached to the former lantern that they did not recognize its later appearance and illumination. Therefore, those who were attached and held tenaciously to the name Abraham were deprived when the Abrahamic virtues reappeared in Moses. Similarly, the Jews were believers in Moses, awaiting the coming of the Messiah. The virtues and perfections of Moses became apparent in Jesus Christ most effulgently, but the Jews held to the name Moses, not adoring the virtues and perfections manifest in Him. Had they been adoring these virtues and seeking these perfections, they would assuredly have believed in Jesus Christ when the same virtues and perfections shone in Him. If we are lovers of the light, we adore it in whatever lamp it may become manifest, but if we love the lamp itself and the light is transferred to another lamp, we will neither accept nor sanction it. Therefore, we must follow and adore the virtues revealed in the Messengers of God – whether in Abraham, Moses, Jesus or other Prophets – but we must not adhere to and adore the lamp.   'Abdu'l-Bahá

♦ Christ was the Prophet of the Christians, Moses of the Jews – why should not the followers of each prophet recognize and honor the other prophets also? If men could only learn the lesson of mutual tolerance, understanding, and brotherly love, the unity of the world would soon be an established fact.

'Abdu'l-Bahá

♦ *Beware of false prophets, which come to you in sheep's clothing, but inwardly they are ravening wolves. Ye shall know them by their fruits. Do men gather grapes of thorns, or figs of thistles? Even so every good tree bringeth forth good fruit; but a corrupt tree bringeth forth evil fruit. A good tree cannot bring forth evil fruit, neither can a corrupt tree bring forth good fruit. Every tree that bringeth not forth good fruit is hewn down, and cast into the fire. Wherefore by their fruits ye shall know them.*

Matthew 7:15-20

Bahá'u'lláh Brings a New Message

♦ ...Praise be to God that thou hast attained!... Thou hast come to see a prisoner and an exile.... We desire but the good of the world and happiness of the nations; yet they deem us a stirrer up of strife and sedition worthy of bondage and banishment.... That all nations should become one in faith and all men as brothers; that the bonds of affection and unity between the sons of men should be strengthened; that diversity of religion should cease, and differences of race be annulled – what harm is there in this?... Yet so it shall be; these fruitless strifes, these ruinous wars shall pass away, and the "Most Great Peace" shall come... Do not you in Europe need this also? Is not this that which Christ foretold?... Yet do we see your kings and rulers lavishing their treasures more freely on means for the destruction of the human race than on that which would conduce to the happiness of mankind.... These strifes and this bloodshed and discord must cease, and all men be as one kindred and one family.... Let not a man glory in this, that he loves his country; let him rather glory in this, that he loves his kind....   *Bahá'u'lláh*

♦ The world's equilibrium hath been upset through the vibrating influence of this most great, this new World Order. Mankind's ordered life hath been revolutionized through the agency of this unique, this wondrous System – the like of which mortal eyes have never witnessed.   *Bahá'u'lláh*

ENVISIONING THE FUTURE

♦ A new life is, in this age, stirring within all the peoples of the earth; and yet none hath discovered its cause or perceived its motive.

Bahá'u'lláh

♦ The world of humanity shall become the manifestation of the lights of Divinity, and the bestowals of God shall surround all. From the standpoints of both material and spiritual civilization extraordinary progress and development will be witnessed. In this present cycle there will be an evolution in civilization unparalleled in the history of the world. The world of humanity has, heretofore, been in the stage of infancy; now it is approaching maturity. Just as the individual human organism, having attained the period of maturity, reaches its fullest degree of physical strength and ripened intellectual faculties so that in one year of this ripened period there is witnessed an unprecedented measure of development, likewise the world of humanity in this cycle of its completeness and consummation will realize an immeasurable upward progress, and that power of accomplishment whereof each individual human reality is the depository of God — that outworking Universal Spirit — like the intellectual faculty, will reveal itself in infinite degrees of perfection.

Therefore, thank ye God that ye have come into the plane of existence in this radiant century wherein the bestowals of God are appearing from all directions, when the doors of the Kingdom have been

opened unto you, the call of God is being raised, and the virtues of the human world are in the process of unfoldment. The day has come when all darkness is to be dispelled, and the Sun of Truth shall shine forth radiantly. This time of the world may be likened to the equinoctial in the annual cycle. For, verily, this is the spring season of God. In the Holy Books a promise is given that the springtime of God shall make itself manifest; Jerusalem, the Holy City, shall descend from heaven; Zion shall leap forth and dance; and the Holy Land shall be submerged in the ocean of divine effulgence.
'Abdu'l-Bahá

♦ Who can doubt that such a consummation — the coming of age of the human race — must signalize, in its turn, the inauguration of a world civilization such as no mortal eye hath ever beheld or human mind conceived? Who is it that can imagine the lofty standard which such a civilization, as it unfolds itself, is destined to attain? Who can measure the heights to which human intelligence, liberated from its shackles, will soar? Who can visualize the realms which the human spirit, vitalized by the outpouring light of Bahá'u'lláh, shining in the plenitude of its glory, will discover?
Shoghi Effendi [1]

---

[1] Bahá'u'lláh's great-grandson

A SELECTION OF BAHÁ'Í PRAYERS

For Spiritual Qualities

Create in me a pure heart, O my God, and renew a tranquil conscience within me, O my Hope! Through the spirit of power confirm Thou me in Thy Cause, O my Best-Beloved, and by the light of Thy glory reveal unto me Thy path, O Thou the Goal of my desire! Through the power of Thy transcendent might lift me up unto the heaven of Thy holiness, O Source of my being, and by the breezes of Thine eternity gladden me, O Thou Who art my God! Let Thine everlasting melodies breathe tranquillity on me, O my Companion, and let the riches of Thine ancient countenance deliver me from all except Thee, O my Master, and let the tidings of the revelation of Thine incorruptible Essence bring me joy, O Thou Who art the most manifest of the manifest and the most hidden of the hidden!

Bahá'u'lláh

For Aid and Assistance

O my God! I ask Thee, by Thy most glorious Name, to aid me in that which will cause the affairs of Thy servants to prosper, and Thy cities to flourish. Thou, indeed, hast power over all things!

Bahá'u'lláh

Daily Prayer

I bear witness, O my God, that Thou hast created me to know Thee and to worship Thee. I testify, at this moment, to my powerlessness and to Thy might, to my poverty and to Thy wealth.

There is none other God but Thee, the Help in Peril, the Self-Subsisting.

Bahá'u'lláh

For Healing

Thy name is my healing, O my God, and remembrance of Thee is my remedy. Nearness to Thee is my hope, and love for Thee is my companion. Thy mercy to me is my healing and my succor in both this world and the world to come. Thou, verily, art the All-Bountiful, the All-Knowing, the All-Wise.

Bahá'u'lláh

For Unity

O my God! O my God! Unite the hearts of Thy servants, and reveal to them Thy great purpose. May they follow Thy commandments and abide in Thy law. Help them, O God, in their endeavor, and grant them strength to serve Thee. O God! Leave them not to themselves, but guide their steps by the light of Thy knowledge, and cheer their hearts by Thy love. Verily, Thou art their Helper and their Lord.

Bahá'u'lláh

For Unity

God grant that the light of unity may envelop the whole earth, and that the seal, "the Kingdom is God's," may be stamped upon the brow of all its peoples.

Bahá'u'lláh

For Love of God

Magnified be Thy name, O Lord my God! Thou art He Whom all things worship and Who worshipeth no one, Who is the Lord of all things and is the vassal of none, Who knoweth all things and is known of none. Thou didst wish to make Thyself known unto men; therefore, Thou didst, through a word of Thy mouth, bring creation into being and fashion the universe. There is none other God except Thee, the Fashioner, the Creator, the Almighty, the Most Powerful.

I implore Thee, by this very word that hath shone forth above the horizon of Thy will, to enable me to drink deep of the living waters through which Thou hast vivified the hearts of Thy chosen ones and quickened the souls of them that love Thee, that I may, at all times and under all conditions, turn my face wholly towards Thee.

Thou art the God of power, of glory and bounty. No God is there beside Thee, the Supreme Ruler, the All-Glorious, the Omniscient.

Bahá'u'lláh

For Aid and Assistance

O God! O God! This is a broken-winged bird and his flight is very slow — assist him so that he may fly toward the apex of prosperity and salvation, wing his way with the utmost joy and happiness throughout the illimitable space, raise his melody in Thy Supreme Name in all the regions, exhilarate the ears with this call, and brighten the eyes by beholding the signs of guidance.

O Lord! I am single, alone and lowly. For me there is no support save Thee, no helper except Thee and no sustainer beside Thee. Confirm me in Thy service, assist me with the cohorts of Thy angels, make me victorious in the promotion of Thy Word and suffer me to speak out Thy wisdom amongst Thy creatures. Verily, Thou art the helper of the weak and the defender of the little ones, and verily Thou art the Powerful, the Mighty and the Unconstrained.

'Abdu'l-Bahá

For the Education of Children

O God! Educate these children. These children are the plants of Thine orchard, the flowers of Thy meadow, the roses of Thy garden. Let Thy rain fall upon them; let the Sun of Reality shine upon them with Thy love. Let Thy breeze refresh them in order that they may be trained, grow and develop, and appear in the utmost beauty. Thou art the Giver. Thou art the Compassionate.

'Abdu'l-Bahá

For the Protection of Children

O Thou kind Lord! These lovely children are the handiwork of the fingers of Thy might and the wondrous signs of Thy greatness. O God! Protect these children, graciously assist them to be educated and enable them to render service to the world of humanity. O God! These children are pearls, cause them to be nurtured within the shell of Thy loving-kindness.

Thou art the Bountiful, the All-Loving.

'Abdu'l-Bahá

For Grace

Lord! Pitiful are we, grant us Thy favor; poor, bestow upon us a share from the ocean of Thy wealth; needy, do Thou satisfy us; abased, give us Thy glory. The fowls of the air and the beasts of the field receive their meat each day from Thee, and all beings partake of Thy care and loving-kindness.

Deprive not this feeble one of Thy wondrous grace and vouchsafe by Thy might unto this helpless soul Thy bounty.

Give us our daily bread, and grant Thine increase in the necessities of life, that we may be dependent on none other but Thee, may commune wholly with Thee, may walk in Thy ways and declare Thy mysteries. Thou art the Almighty and the Loving and the Provider of all mankind.

'Abdu'l-Bahá

For Humanity

O Thou kind Lord! Thou hast created all humanity from the same stock. Thou hast decreed that all shall belong to the same household. In Thy Holy Presence they are all Thy servants, and all mankind are sheltered beneath Thy Tabernacle; all have gathered together at Thy Table of Bounty; all are illumined through the light of Thy Providence.

O God! Thou art kind to all, Thou hast provided for all, dost shelter all, conferrest life upon all. Thou hast endowed each and all with talents and faculties, and all are submerged in the Ocean of Thy Mercy.

O Thou kind Lord! Unite all. Let the religions agree and make the nations one, so that they may see each other as one family and the whole earth as one home. May they all live together in perfect harmony.

O God! Raise aloft the banner of the oneness of mankind.

O God! Establish the Most Great Peace.

Cement Thou, O God, the hearts together.

O Thou kind Father, God! Gladden our hearts through the fragrance of Thy love. Brighten our eyes through the Light of Thy Guidance. Delight our ears with the melody of Thy Word, and shelter us all in the Stronghold of Thy Providence.

Thou art the Mighty and Powerful, Thou art the Forgiving and Thou art the One Who overlooketh the shortcomings of all mankind.

'Abdu'l-Bahá

Where to from here?

The weight of the potentialities with which this Faith, possessing no peer or equal in the world's spiritual history, and marking the culmination of a universal prophetic cycle, has been endowed, staggers our imagination. The brightness of the millennial glory which it must shed in the fullness of time dazzles our eyes. The magnitude of the shadow which its Author will continue to cast on successive Prophets destined to be raised up after Him eludes our calculation.

— Shoghi Effendi

For more information about the Bahá'í Faith, check your local White Pages under "Baha'i" or call:

1-800-22-UNITE

Additional information can be found at:

http://www.bahai.org *or*

http://www.us.bahai.org